Celebrations

Publications International, Ltd.

Every recipe was developed and tested in the Campbell Soup Company Global Consumer Food Center by professional home economists.

Front cover photography by Campbell Soup Company Creative Photography Studio.

All other photography:
Photography: Sacco Studio Limited, Chicago
Photographer: Tom O'Connell
Photo Stylist: Paula M. Walters
Food Stylists: Gail O'Donnell, Dianne Hugh
Assistant Food Stylist: Liza Brown

Pictured on the front cover: Ham & Cheese Stromboli *(page 74)*, Vegetable Tortilla Triangles *(page 90)*, Mini Cheese-Tomato Napoleons *(page 61)* and Party Meatballs *(page 68)*.

Pictured on the back cover *(top to bottom):* French Toast Casserole *(page 30)*, Beef Taco Bake *(page 78)* and Tomato Soup Spice Cake *(page 76)*.

ISBN: 0-7853-3591-9

Manufactured in U.S.A.

8 7 6 5 4 3 2 1

Nutritional Analysis: Values are approximate; calculations are based upon food composition data in the Campbell Soup Company Master Data Base. Some variation in nutrition values may result from periodic product changes. Each analysis is based on the food items in the ingredient list, excluding optional ingredients and garnishes. When a choice is given for an ingredient, calculations are based upon the first choice listed.

Microwave Cooking: Microwave ovens vary in wattage. Use the cooking times as guidelines and check for doneness before adding more time.

Preparation/Cooking Times: Preparation times are based on the approximate amount of time required to assemble the recipe before cooking, baking or chilling. These times include preparation steps such as measuring, chopping and mixing. The fact that some preparations and cooking can be done simultaneously is taken into account. Preparation of optional ingredients and serving suggestions is not included.

Campbell's

Celebrations

Campbell's
QUICK MEALS
FOR BUSY DAYS

Asian Turkey Stir-Fry

Prep Time: 5 minutes   **Cook Time:** 20 minutes

- 1 tablespoon vegetable oil
- 1 bag (16 ounces) any frozen vegetable combination, thawed
- 1 can (10¾ ounces) CAMPBELL'S Condensed Golden Mushroom Soup
- 3 tablespoons soy sauce
- 1 teaspoon garlic powder
- 2 cups cubed cooked turkey *or* chicken
- 4 cups hot cooked rice

1. In medium skillet over medium heat, heat oil. Add vegetables and stir-fry until tender-crisp.

2. Add soup, soy sauce and garlic powder. Heat to a boil. Add turkey and heat through. Serve over rice.   *Serves 4*

TIP

To thaw vegetables, microwave on HIGH 3 minutes.

Asian Turkey Stir-Fry

Baked Onion Chicken

Prep Time: 10 minutes   **Cook Time:** 20 minutes

1 pouch CAMPBELL'S Dry Onion Soup and Recipe Mix
⅔ cup dry bread crumbs *or* cracker crumbs
⅛ teaspoon pepper
1 egg *or* 2 egg whites
2 tablespoons water
6 skinless, boneless chicken breast halves *or* 12 skinless, boneless chicken thighs (about 1½ pounds)
2 tablespoons margarine *or* butter, melted (optional)

1. Crush soup mix in pouch with rolling pin. Mix soup mix, bread crumbs and pepper on plate.

2. Mix egg and water in shallow dish. Dip chicken into egg mixture. Coat with crumb mixture.

3. Place chicken on baking sheet. Drizzle with margarine. Bake at 400°F. for 20 minutes or until chicken is no longer pink.

Serves 6

TIP

For ⅔ cup cracker crumbs,
finely crush 16 saltine crackers.

Clockwise from top: *Green Bean Bake (page 55),
Baked Onion Chicken and Cheddar Mashed Potato Bake (page 54)*

Skillet Fiesta Chicken & Rice

Prep Time: 5 minutes   **Cook Time:** 20 minutes

>   1 tablespoon vegetable oil
>   4 skinless, boneless chicken breast halves (about
>   1 pound)
>   1 can (10¾ ounces) CAMPBELL'S Condensed Tomato
>   Soup
>   1⅓ cups water
>   1 teaspoon chili powder
>   1½ cups *uncooked* Minute® Original Rice
>   ¼ cup shredded Cheddar cheese (1 ounce)

1. In medium skillet over medium-high heat, heat oil. Add chicken and cook 10 minutes or until browned. Set chicken aside. Pour off fat.

2. Add soup, water and chili powder. Heat to a boil.

3. Stir in rice. Place chicken on rice mixture. Sprinkle chicken with additional chili powder and cheese. Reduce heat to low. Cover and cook 5 minutes or until chicken and rice are done. Stir rice mixture.

Serves 4

TIP

Always be sure to cook chicken thoroughly, to a minimum internal temperature of 165°F.

Skillet Fiesta Chicken & Rice

Shortcut Chicken Cordon Bleu

Prep Time: 10 minutes   **Cook Time:** 20 minutes

> 1 tablespoon margarine *or* butter
> 4 skinless, boneless chicken breast halves (about
>   1 pound)
> 1 can (10¾ ounces) CAMPBELL'S Condensed Cream
>   of Chicken Soup *or* 98% Fat Free Cream of
>   Chicken Soup
> 2 tablespoons water
> 2 tablespoons Chablis *or other dry white wine*
> ½ cup shredded Swiss cheese (2 ounces)
> ½ cup chopped cooked ham
> 4 cups hot cooked medium egg noodles (about
>   3 cups uncooked)

1. In medium skillet over medium-high heat, heat margarine. Add chicken and cook 10 minutes or until browned. Set chicken aside.

2. Add soup, water, wine, cheese and ham. Heat to a boil, stirring often. Return chicken to pan. Reduce heat to low. Cover and cook 5 minutes or until chicken is no longer pink, stirring occasionally. Serve with noodles.   *Serves 4*

TIP

Store uncooked chicken in the coldest part of your refrigerator for no more than 2 days before cooking.

Shortcut Chicken Cordon Bleu

Turkey with a Twist

Prep Time: 5 minutes   **Cook Time:** 20 minutes

   1 can (10¾ ounces) CAMPBELL'S Condensed
       Cheddar Cheese Soup
  ¼ cup milk
   1 cup PACE Picante Sauce *or* Thick & Chunky Salsa
  ½ teaspoon garlic powder *or* 2 cloves garlic, minced
   1 can (about 8 ounces) whole kernel corn, drained
1½ cups cubed cooked turkey *or* chicken
   4 cups cooked corkscrew macaroni (3 cups
       uncooked)

In large saucepan mix soup, milk, picante sauce, garlic powder, corn, turkey and macaroni. Over low heat, heat through.   *Serves 4*

TIP

No cooked poultry on hand? Substitute 2 cans
(5 ounces **each**) SWANSON Premium Chunk
Chicken Breast **or** Chunk Chicken for 1½ cups
cooked turkey or chicken.

Turkey with a Twist

Guilt-Free Alfredo

Prep Time: 10 minutes   **Cook Time:** 15 minutes

> 1 can (14½ ounces) SWANSON Chicken Broth
>   (1¾ cups)
> ¼ cup all-purpose flour
> ¼ teaspoon garlic powder *or* 2 cloves garlic, minced
> ¼ teaspoon pepper
> ⅓ cup plain yogurt
> 6 cups hot cooked linguine (about 12 ounces
>   uncooked), cooked without salt
> 6 tablespoons grated Parmesan cheese
>   Chopped fresh parsley

1. In medium saucepan gradually mix broth into flour, garlic powder and pepper until smooth. Over medium heat, cook until mixture boils and thickens, stirring constantly.

2. Remove from heat. Stir in yogurt. Toss with pasta and **4 tablespoons** cheese. Sprinkle with parsley and remaining cheese.

Serves 6

Note: 3g fat per serving
(traditional Fetuccine Alfredo recipe: 17g fat per serving)

Guilt-Free Alfredo

Quick Skillet Ziti

Prep Time: 10 minutes   **Cook Time:** 15 minutes

    1 pound ground beef
    1 jar (28 ounces) PREGO Traditional Pasta Sauce
    5 cups cooked medium tube-shaped macaroni (about
        3 cups uncooked)
    Grated Parmesan cheese

1. In medium skillet over medium-high heat, cook beef until browned, stirring to separate meat. Pour off fat.

2. Add pasta sauce and macaroni. Reduce heat to low and heat through. Serve with cheese.   *Serves 5*

TIP

For a shortcut supper on a busy day, try PREGO Spaghetti & Meatballs. In a large saucepan mix 1 jar (28 ounces) PREGO Traditional Pasta Sauce with 12 frozen *or* refrigerated fully cooked meatballs (about 12 ounces). Over medium heat, heat to a boil. Reduce heat to low. Cover and cook about 15 minutes or until meatballs are heated through, stirring occasionally. Serve over 4 cups hot cooked spaghetti (about 8 ounces uncooked). *Serves 4*

Quick Skillet Ziti

Country Beef & Vegetables

Prep Time: 5 minutes   **Cook Time:** 20 minutes

    1½ pounds ground beef
      1 can (26 ounces) CAMPBELL'S Condensed Tomato
        Soup
      1 tablespoon Worcestershire sauce
      1 bag (16 ounces) frozen mixed vegetables
      6 cups hot cooked rice
        Shredded Cheddar cheese

1. In medium skillet over medium-high heat, cook beef until browned, stirring to separate meat. Pour off fat.

2. Add soup, Worcestershire and vegetables. Heat to a boil. Reduce heat to low. Cook 5 minutes or until vegetables are tender. Serve over rice. Top with cheese.   *Serves 6*

TIP

Always cook ground meat thoroughly,
to a minimum temperature of 155°F.

Country Beef & Vegetables

BRUNCHES & BUFFETS

Classic Campbelled Eggs

Prep Time: 10 minutes   **Cook Time:** 15 minutes

> 1 can (10¾ ounces) CAMPBELL'S Condensed Cheddar Cheese Soup
> 8 eggs, beaten
>   Dash pepper
> 2 tablespoons margarine *or* butter
>   Chopped fresh parsley for garnish

1. In medium bowl mix soup, eggs and pepper.

2. In medium skillet over low heat, heat margarine. Add egg mixture. As eggs begin to set, stir lightly so uncooked egg mixture flows to bottom. Cook until set but still moist. Garnish with parsley.

Serves 4

Top to bottom: *Ham and Cheese Hash Browns (page 26) and Classic Campbelled Eggs*

Breakfast Tacos

Prep Time: 15 minutes   **Cook Time:** 10 minutes

1 tablespoon margarine *or* butter
1 medium potato, cooked and diced (about 1 cup)
4 eggs, beaten
4 slices bacon, cooked and crumbled
4 flour tortillas (8-inch)
¾ cup shredded Cheddar cheese (3 ounces)
½ cup PACE Picante Sauce *or* Thick & Chunky Salsa

1. In medium skillet over medium heat, heat margarine. Add potato and cook until lightly browned. Add eggs and bacon and cook until eggs are set but still moist.

2. Warm tortillas according to package directions. Spoon about *½ cup* potato mixture down center of each tortilla. Top with cheese and picante sauce. Roll up.   *Makes 4 tacos*

TIP

To add zest to breakfast and brunch food, "Pour on the PACE" Salsa or Picante Sauce over scrambled eggs, omelets, home fries and hash browns!

Top to bottom: *Picante Brunch Quiche (page 27) and Breakfast Taco*

Ham & Cheese Hash Browns

(photo on page 23)

Prep Time: 10 minutes   **Cook Time:** 20 minutes

    1 tablespoon margarine *or* butter
    ½ cup chopped cooked ham
    1 medium onion, sliced (about ½ cup)
    ¼ cup diced green *or* sweet red pepper
    1 can (10¾ ounces) CAMPBELL'S Condensed
        Cheddar Cheese Soup *or* Condensed Broccoli
        Cheese Soup
    ½ cup milk
    1 teaspoon prepared mustard
    4 cups frozen diced potatoes (hash browns)

1. In medium skillet over medium heat, heat margarine. Add ham, onion and pepper and cook until vegetables are tender-crisp.

2. Add soup, milk, mustard and potatoes. Heat to a boil. Reduce heat to low. Cover and cook 10 minutes or until potatoes are tender, stirring often.   *Serves 6*

TIP

These creamy hash browns also make a delicious dinner side dish with ham, beef or chicken!

Picante Brunch Quiche

(photo on page 25)

Prep Time: 10 minutes   **Cook/Stand Time:** 45 minutes

　　　1 cup shredded Cheddar cheese (4 ounces)
　　　4 slices bacon, cooked and crumbled
　　　2 green onions, sliced (about ¼ cup)
　　　1 (9-inch) frozen pie crust
　　　½ cup PACE Picante Sauce *or* Thick & Chunky Salsa
　　　3 eggs, beaten
　　　½ cup half-and-half *or* milk

1. Preheat oven to 350°F.

2. Arrange cheese, bacon and onions in pie crust. Mix picante sauce, eggs and half-and-half. Pour over cheese mixture.

3. Bake 35 minutes or until crust is golden and knife inserted in center comes out clean. Let stand 10 minutes. Serve with additional picante sauce.

Serves 6

TIP

For convenience use packaged pre-shredded Cheddar cheese. Half an 8-ounce package will provide the 1 cup needed for this recipe.

Brunch Ham Puffs

Bake/Prep Time: 45 minutes   **Cook Time:** 10 minutes

   1 package (10 ounces) PEPPERIDGE FARM Frozen
      Puff Pastry Shells
   1 can (10¾ ounces) CAMPBELL'S Condensed Cream
      of Chicken Soup *or* 98% Fat Free Cream of
      Chicken Soup
   ½ cup milk
   1 teaspoon Dijon-style mustard
  1½ cups cubed cooked ham
  1½ cups cooked asparagus cut in 1-inch pieces
   ½ cup shredded Swiss cheese (2 ounces)

1. Bake pastry shells according to package directions.

2. In medium saucepan mix soup, milk, mustard, ham, asparagus and cheese. Over medium heat, heat through, stirring often.

3. Serve in pastry shells.

Serves 6

TIP

Always bake pastry shells in a preheated 400°F. oven, for 20 to 25 minutes or until golden brown. **Do not bake in a microwave or a toaster oven.** Unfilled baked shells may be stored in an airtight container at room temperature for up to 2 days.

Brunch Ham Puffs

French Toast Casserole

Prep/Chill Time: 1 hour 15 minutes   **Cook Time:** 50 minutes

1 loaf (16 ounces) PEPPERIDGE FARM Cinnamon
  Swirl Bread, any variety, cut into cubes (about
  8 cups)
6 eggs
3 cups milk
2 teaspoons vanilla extract
Confectioners' sugar

1. In greased 3-quart shallow baking dish arrange bread cubes. Mix eggs, milk and vanilla. Pour over bread. Cover and refrigerate 1 hour or overnight.

2. Uncover. Bake at 350°F. for 50 minutes or until golden. Sprinkle with confectioners' sugar. *Serve with pancake syrup if desired.*

Serves 8

TIP

This quick-to-assemble breakfast casserole can be refrigerated overnight for a special morning treat.

French Toast Casserole

Cinnamon-Raisin Loaves

Prep Time: 20 minutes   **Bake Time:** 55 minutes

Vegetable cooking spray
3 cups all-purpose flour
2 teaspoons ground cinnamon
1 teaspoon baking soda
½ teaspoon baking powder
1½ cups sugar
1 can (10¾ ounces) CAMPBELL'S HEALTHY REQUEST
    Condensed Tomato Soup
6 egg whites
⅓ cup vegetable oil
1 teaspoon vanilla extract
2 small zucchini, shredded (about 2 cups)
1 cup raisins

1. Preheat oven to 350°F. Spray two 8½- by 4½-inch loaf pans with cooking spray. Set aside.

2. Mix flour, cinnamon, baking soda and baking powder. Set aside.

3. Mix sugar, soup, egg whites, oil and vanilla. Add to flour mixture, stirring just to moisten. Fold in zucchini and raisins. Pour into prepared pans.

4. Bake in center of oven 55 minutes or until toothpick inserted in center comes out clean. Cool in pans on wire rack 10 minutes. Remove from pans and cool completely on rack.   *Serves 24*

Nutritional Values per Serving: Calories 170, Total Fat 3g, Saturated Fat 1g, Cholesterol 0mg, Sodium 119mg, Total Carbohydrate 32g, Protein 3g

Cinnamon-Raisin Loaves

Grilled Chicken Caesar Salad

Prep/Marinating Time: 25 minutes   **Cook Time:** 15 minutes

Dressing/Marinade
- 1 can (10¾ ounces) CAMPBELL'S HEALTHY REQUEST Condensed Cream of Chicken Soup
- ½ cup water
- 2 tablespoons cider vinegar
- 2 tablespoons lemon juice
- 2 teaspoons Worcestershire sauce
- 4 cloves garlic, minced *or* ½ teaspoon garlic powder
- ½ teaspoon freshly ground pepper
- 4 tablespoons grated Parmesan cheese

Salad
- 4 skinless, boneless chicken breast halves (about 1 pound)
- 1 large head romaine lettuce torn into bite-size pieces (about 12 cups)
- ½ cup PEPPERIDGE FARM Fat Free Caesar Croutons

1. In large shallow nonmetallic dish mix soup, water, vinegar, lemon juice, Worcestershire, garlic, pepper and *3 tablespoons* cheese. Set aside *1¼ cups* for dressing. Add chicken to remaining soup mixture in dish and turn to coat. Cover and refrigerate 15 minutes.

2. Remove chicken from soup mixture and place on rack in broiler pan. Broil 4 inches from heat 15 minutes or until chicken is no longer pink, turning and brushing often with soup mixture. Discard any remaining soup mixture. Slice chicken into thin strips.

3. In large bowl toss lettuce, chicken and dressing until evenly coated. Sprinkle with croutons and remaining cheese.

Serves 6

Nutritional Values per Serving: Calories 206, Total Fat 4g, Saturated Fat 2g, Cholesterol 55mg, Sodium 457mg, Total Carbohydrate 16g, Protein 23g

Top to bottom: Confetti Risotto (page 40) and Grilled Chicken Caesar Salad

Broccoli Cheese Tart

Prep/Cook Time: 1 hour   **Stand Time:** 5 minutes

½ cup shredded Cheddar cheese (2 ounces)
¼ cup shredded Monterey Jack cheese (1 ounce)
¼ cup shredded mozzarella cheese (1 ounce)
1 can (10¾ ounces) CAMPBELL'S Condensed Broccoli
　　Cheese Soup *or* 98% Fat Free Broccoli Cheese
　　Soup
5 eggs
¼ teaspoon garlic powder *or* 2 cloves garlic, minced
1 package (10 ounces) frozen chopped broccoli
　　(2 cups), thawed and drained
1 small onion, finely chopped (about ¼ cup)
1 (9-inch) baked deep dish pie crust

1. Mix Cheddar cheese, Monterey Jack cheese and mozzarella cheese. Set aside.

2. In medium bowl mix soup, eggs, garlic powder, broccoli, onion and ½ *cup* cheese mixture. Pour into prepared pie crust.

3. Bake at 350°F. for 45 minutes or until knife inserted in center comes out clean. Sprinkle remaining cheese around edge of tart. Bake 5 minutes more. Let stand 5 minutes.   *Serves 6 to 8*

TIP

To thaw broccoli, microwave on HIGH 4 minutes.

Broccoli Cheese Tart

Easy Party Lasagna

Prep Time: 20 minutes   **Cook/Stand Time:** 1 hour

    1 can (10¾ ounces) CAMPBELL'S Condensed Cream of Mushroom Soup *or* 98% Fat Free Cream of Mushroom Soup
    ¼ cup milk
    2 cups shredded mozzarella cheese (8 ounces)
    1 pound ground beef
    1 can (11⅛ ounces) CAMPBELL'S Condensed Italian Tomato Soup
    1 cup water
    6 *uncooked* lasagna noodles

1. Mix mushroom soup, milk and **½ cup** cheese. Set aside.

2. In medium skillet over medium-high heat, cook beef until browned, stirring to separate meat. Pour off fat. Stir in Italian tomato soup and water. Heat through.

3. In 2-quart shallow baking dish spoon **half** the meat mixture. Top with **3** lasagna noodles and mushroom soup mixture. Top with remaining **3** lasagna noodles and remaining meat mixture.

4. Cover. Bake at 400°F. for 40 minutes or until hot. Uncover and sprinkle remaining cheese over top. Bake 10 minutes more or until hot and cheese is melted. Let stand 10 minutes.

Serves 8

Top to bottom: *Easy Party Lasagna and Vegetable Lasagna (page 41)*

Creamy Risotto

Prep Time: 5 minutes   **Cook/Stand Time:** 15 minutes

> 1 can (10¾ ounces) CAMPBELL'S HEALTHY REQUEST
> Condensed Cream of Mushroom Soup
> 1½ cups CAMPBELL'S HEALTHY REQUEST Ready to
> Serve Chicken Broth
> 1½ cups *uncooked* Minute® Original Rice
> 1 tablespoon grated Parmesan Cheese

1. In medium saucepan mix soup and broth. Over medium-high heat, heat to a boil.

2. Stir in rice and cheese. Cover and remove from heat. Let stand 10 minutes. Fluff with fork. Serve with freshly ground pepper and additional Parmesan cheese, if desired.   *Serves 4*

Nutritional Values per Serving: Calories 190, Total Fat 2g, Saturated Fat 1g, Cholesterol 7mg, Sodium 480mg, Total Carborhydrate 36g, Protein 4g

Confetti Risotto (photo on page 35): In step 1 add ¼ teaspoon dried thyme leaves, crushed, ½ cup frozen peas, 1 small carrot, shredded (about ⅓ cup) and 1 small onion, finely chopped (about ¼ cup) with soup and broth. Proceed as in step 2. *Serves 4*

Nutritional Values per Serving: Calories 214, Total Fat 2g, Saturated Fat 1g, Cholesterol 7mg, Sodium 513mg, Total Carbohydrate 40mg, Protein 6mg.

Tomato-Basil Risotto: In step 2 add 1 tablespoon chopped fresh basil *or* ¼ teaspoon dried basil leaves, crushed, and 1 small tomato, diced (about ½ cup), *or* ½ cup drained cut-up canned tomatoes with rice. *Serves 4*

Nutritional Values per Serving: Calories 197, Total Fat 2g, Saturated Fat 1g, Cholesterol 7mg, Sodium 492mg, Total Carbohydrate 38g, Protein 5g

Vegetable Lasagna

(photo on page 39)

Prep Time: 20 minutes   **Cook/Stand Time:** 40 minutes

> 1 package (10 ounces) frozen chopped broccoli
> 1 small red *or* green pepper, chopped (about ½ cup)
> 1 medium carrot, chopped (about ⅓ cup)
> 1 small onion, chopped (about ¼ cup)
> 1 can (10¾ ounces) CAMPBELL'S Condensed Broccoli Cheese Soup *or* 98% Fat Free Broccoli Cheese Soup
> ½ cup milk
> ¼ cup grated Parmesan cheese
> 6 lasagna noodles, cooked and drained
> 1½ cups shredded mozzarella cheese (6 ounces)

1. In medium saucepan place broccoli, pepper, carrot and onion. Cover with water. Over medium-high heat, heat to a boil. Reduce heat to low. Cover and cook 5 minutes or until tender. Drain.

2. Mix soup, milk and Parmesan cheese. Set aside.

3. In 2-quart shallow baking dish spread *½ cup* soup mixture. Top with *3* lasagna noodles, *½ cup* soup mixture, *¾ cup* mozzarella cheese and *1½ cups* vegetable mixture. Repeat layers. Top with remaining soup mixture.

4. Bake at 400°F. for 20 minutes. Uncover and bake 10 minutes more or until hot. Let stand 10 minutes.   *Serves 6*

Tuna Noodle Casserole

Prep Time: 15 minutes   **Cook Time:** 25 minutes

1 can (10¾ ounces) CAMPBELL'S Condensed Cream
   of Mushroom Soup *or* 98% Fat Free Cream of
   Mushroom Soup
½ cup milk
2 tablespoons chopped pimiento (optional)
1 cup cooked peas
2 cans (about 6 ounces *each*) tuna, drained and
   flaked
2 cups hot cooked medium egg noodles (about
   1 cup uncooked)
2 tablespoons dry bread crumbs
1 tablespoon margarine *or* butter, melted

1. In 1½-quart casserole mix soup, milk, pimiento, peas, tuna and noodles. Bake at 400°F. for 20 minutes or until hot.

2. Stir. Mix bread crumbs with margarine and sprinkle over noodle mixture. Bake 5 minutes more.   *Serves 4*

TIP

For a cheesy bread topping, mix ¼ cup shredded
Cheddar cheese (about 1 ounce) with bread crumbs
and margarine. For a change of taste, substitute
1 can (10¾ ounces) CAMPBELL'S Condensed Cream
of Celery Soup **or** 98% Fat Free Cream of Celery
Soup for Cream of Mushroom Soup.

Tuna Noodle Casserole

Turkey Broccoli Divan

Prep Time: 15 minutes   **Cook Time:** 25 minutes

1 pound fresh broccoli, cut into spears, cooked and
    drained, *or* 1 package (about 10 ounces) frozen
    broccoli spears, cooked and drained
1½ cups cubed cooked turkey *or* chicken
1 can (10¾ ounces) CAMPBELL'S Condensed Broccoli
    Cheese Soup *or* Cream of Chicken Soup
⅓ cup milk
½ cup shredded Cheddar cheese (2 ounces, optional)
2 tablespoons dry bread crumbs
1 tablespoon margarine *or* butter, melted

1. In 9-inch pie plate *or* 2-quart shallow baking dish arrange broccoli and turkey. In small bowl mix soup and milk and pour over broccoli and turkey.

2. Sprinkle cheese over soup mixture. Mix bread crumbs with margarine and sprinkle over cheese.

3. Bake at 400°F. for 25 minutes or until hot.   *Serves 4*

TIP

For a lighter version, substitute 1 can (10¾ ounces)
CAMPBELL'S 98% Fat Free Cream of Chicken Soup.

Turkey Broccoli Divan

Crispy Macaroni & Cheese

Prep Time: 20 minutes   **Cook Time:** 20 minutes

> 1 can (10¾ ounces) CAMPBELL'S Condensed Cream of Mushroom Soup *or* 98% Fat Free Cream of Mushroom Soup
> ½ cup milk
> ½ teaspoon prepared mustard
>   Generous dash pepper
> 2 cups shredded Cheddar cheese (8 ounces)
> 3 cups hot cooked elbow macaroni (about 1½ cups uncooked)
> 1 can (2.8 ounces) French fried onions (1⅓ cups)

1. In 1½-quart casserole mix soup, milk, mustard, pepper, *1½ cups* cheese and macaroni. Bake at 400°F. for 20 minutes or until hot.

2. Stir. Sprinkle onions and remaining cheese over top. Bake 1 minute more or until onions are golden.   *Serves 4*

TIP

To double recipe, double all ingredients. Use 3-quart shallow baking dish. *Serves 8*

Top to bottom: *Ranchero Macaroni Bake (page 51) and Crispy Macaroni & Cheese*

German Potato Salad

10 medium potatoes (about 3 pounds)
 1 can (14½ ounces) SWANSON Beef Broth
 ¼ cup all-purpose flour
 3 tablespoons sugar
 ½ teaspoon celery seed
 ½ teaspoon salt
 ⅛ teaspoon pepper
 ¼ cup cider vinegar
 1 medium onion, chopped (about ½ cup)
 3 tablespoons chopped fresh parsley

1. In Dutch oven place potatoes. Cover with water. Over high heat, heat to a boil. Cook 20 minutes or until tender. Drain. Cut into cubes.

2. In medium saucepan gradually mix broth into flour, sugar, celery seed, salt and pepper until smooth. Add vinegar and onion. Over medium heat, cook until mixture boils and thickens, stirring constantly. Reduce heat to low. Cook 5 minutes or until onion is tender.

3. In large bowl toss potatoes, parsley and broth mixture until evenly coated.

Serves 12

Note: 0g fat per serving

TIP

Use round white *or* red potatoes that have a firm, waxy texture.

Top to bottom: *German Potato Salad and Basil and Garlic Potatoes (page 50)*

Basil & Garlic Potatoes

(photo on page 49)

Prep Time: 15 minutes   **Cook Time:** 1 hour

11 medium potatoes (about 3½ pounds), thinly sliced
 4 cloves garlic, minced
 2 teaspoons dried basil leaves, crushed
 ¼ teaspoon pepper
 1 can (14½ ounces) SWANSON Chicken Broth
   (1¾ cups)

1. In 3-quart shallow baking dish layer half the potatoes, garlic, basil and pepper. Repeat layers. Pour broth over potato mixture.

2. Bake at 350°F. for 1 hour or until potatoes are tender.

Serves 12

Note: 0g fat per serving

Roasted Garlic Potatoes: In 3-quart shallow baking dish arrange 11 medium potatoes, thinly sliced (about 3½ pounds). Pour 1 can (14½ ounces) SWANSON Seasoned Chicken Broth with Roasted Garlic over potatoes. Cover and bake at 400°F. for 40 minutes. Uncover and bake 15 minutes more or until potatoes are tender.

Serves 12

Note: 0g fat per serving

Ranchero Macaroni Bake

(photo on page 47)
Prep Time: 20 minutes   **Cook Time:** 25 minutes

1 can (26 ounces) CAMPBELL'S Condensed Cream of
  Mushroom Soup *or* 98% Fat Free Cream of
  Mushroom Soup
1 cup milk
1 cup PACE Thick & Chunky Salsa *or* Picante Sauce
3 cups shredded Cheddar *or* Monterey Jack cheese
  (12 ounces)
6 cups hot cooked elbow macaroni (about 3 cups
  uncooked)
1 cup coarsely crushed tortilla chips

1. Mix soup, milk, salsa, cheese and macaroni. Spoon into 3-quart shallow baking dish.

2. Bake at 400°F. for 20 minutes or until hot.

3. Stir. Sprinkle chips over macaroni mixture. Bake 5 minutes more.

Serves 8 as a main dish or 12 as a side dish

Florentine Casserole

Prep Time: 10 minutes   **Cook Time:** 35 minutes

4 cups PEPPERIDGE FARM Herb Seasoned Stuffing
1 tablespoon margarine *or* butter, melted
1 can (10¾ ounces) CAMPBELL'S Condensed Cream of Celery Soup *or* 98% Fat Free Cream of Celery Soup
½ cup sour cream *or* plain yogurt
1 teaspoon onion powder
1 package (about 10 ounces) frozen chopped spinach, thawed
¼ cup grated Parmesan cheese

1. Mix ½ *cup* stuffing and margarine. Set aside.

2. Mix soup, sour cream, onion powder, spinach and cheese. Add remaining stuffing. Mix lightly. Spoon into 1½-quart casserole. Sprinkle reserved stuffing mixture over top.

3. Bake at 350°F. for 35 minutes or until hot.   *Serves 6*

TIP

To thaw spinach, microwave on HIGH 3 minutes, breaking apart with fork halfway through heating.

Florentine Casserole

Cheddar Mashed Potato Bake

(photo on page 9)
Prep Time: 10 minutes   **Cook Time:** 30 minutes

> 1 can (10¾ ounces) CAMPBELL'S Condensed
>   Cheddar Cheese Soup
> ⅓ cup sour cream *or* plain yogurt
>   Generous dash pepper
> 1 green onion, chopped (about 2 tablespoons)
> 3 cups stiff, seasoned mashed potatoes

1. In 1½-quart casserole mix soup, sour cream, pepper and onion. Stir in potatoes.

2. Bake at 350°F. for 30 minutes or until hot.   *Serves 8*

Variation: In small bowl mix 1 tablespoon melted margarine **or** butter, 2 tablespoons dry bread crumbs and ¼ teaspoon paprika. Sprinkle over potato mixture before baking.

TIP

To make 3 cups stiff, seasoned mashed potatoes, in medium saucepan place 2 pounds potatoes, peeled and cut into 1-inch pieces. Cover with water. Add salt if desired. Over high heat, heat to a boil. Reduce heat to medium. Cover and cook 10 minutes or until potatoes are tender. Drain. Mash potatoes with ¾ cup milk and 2 tablespoons margarine **or** butter. Season to taste with salt and pepper.

Green Bean Bake

(photo on page 9)
Prep Time: 10 minutes   **Cook Time:** 30 minutes

1 can (10¾ ounces) CAMPBELL'S Condensed Cream
   of Mushroom Soup *or* 98% Fat Free Cream of
   Mushroom Soup
½ cup milk
1 teaspoon soy sauce
   Dash pepper
4 cups cooked cut green beans
1 can (2.8 ounces) French fried onions (1⅓ cups)

1. In 1½-quart casserole mix soup, milk, soy sauce, pepper, beans
and ½ *can* onions.

2. Bake at 350°F. for 25 minutes or until hot.

3. Stir. Sprinkle remaining onions over bean mixture. Bake 5 minutes
more or until onions are golden.   *Serves 6*

TIP

Use 1 bag (16 to 20 ounces) frozen green beans,
2 packages (9 ounces *each*) frozen green beans,
2 cans (about 16 ounces *each*) green beans *or* about
1½ pounds fresh green beans. To make Green Bean
Bake for a crowd, substitute 1 can (26 ounces)
CAMPBELL'S Condensed Cream of Mushroom Soup
and double all other ingredients. Bake in a 3-quart
shallow baking dish. *Serves 10*

Campbell's
APPETIZERS & SWEETS

Double Cheese Dip

Prep Time: 10 minutes   **Cook Time:** 15 minutes

- 1 cup PACE Picante Sauce *or* Thick & Chunky Salsa
- 1 teaspoon chili powder
- 1 package (8 ounces) cream cheese, softened
- 1 cup shredded Cheddar cheese (4 ounces)
- ¼ cup sliced pitted ripe olives

1. Mix picante sauce and chili powder. Spread cream cheese in 9-inch pie plate. Top with picante sauce mixture, Cheddar cheese, olives and additional picante sauce.

2. Bake at 350°F. for 15 minutes or until hot. Serve with pita triangles, tortilla chips or fresh vegetables for dipping.

Makes about 3 cups

Double Cheese Crab Dip: In step 1, top picante sauce mixture with 1 can (8 ounces) refrigerated pasteurized crab meat, Cheddar cheese, olives and additional picante sauce.

Top to bottom: *Salsa-Ranch Dip (page 60)
and Double Cheese Dip*

Shrimp Dip

Prep Time: 10 minutes   **Chill Time:** 4 hours

1 package (8 ounces) cream cheese, softened
1 can (10¾ ounces) CAMPBELL'S Condensed Cream
   of Shrimp Soup
½ teaspoon Louisiana-style hot sauce
¼ cup finely chopped celery
1 tablespoon finely chopped onion

Stir cream cheese until smooth. Stir in soup, hot sauce, celery and
onion. Refrigerate at least 4 hours. Serve with crackers, chips or
fresh vegetables for dipping.   *Makes 2¼ cups*

Spinach Onion Dip

Prep Time: 10 minutes   **Chill Time:** 2 hours

1 pouch CAMPBELL'S Dry Onion Soup and Recipe
   Mix
1 container (16 ounces) sour cream
1 package (about 10 ounces) frozen chopped
   spinach, thawed and *well drained*
⅓ cup chopped toasted almonds (optional)

Mix soup mix, sour cream, spinach and almonds. Refrigerate at
least 2 hours. Serve with chips or fresh vegetables for dipping.
                                                 Makes 2⅔ cups

Top to bottom: *Spinach Onion Dip
and Shrimp Dip*

Salsa-Ranch Dip

(photo on page 57)
Prep Time: 5 minutes   **Chill Time:** 1 hour

¾ cup PACE Thick & Chunky Salsa *or* Picante Sauce
1 container (16 ounces) sour cream
1 package (1.0 ounce) ranch dip mix

Mix salsa, sour cream and dip mix. Refrigerate at least 1 hour. Serve with chips or fresh vegetables for dipping.   *Makes 2½ cups*

Bloody Mary Mocktail

(photo on page 63)
Prep Time: 5 minutes

3 cups V8 100% Vegetable Juice
1 teaspoon prepared horseradish
1 teaspoon Worcestershire sauce
½ teaspoon hot pepper sauce
Lemon slices for garnish

Mix vegetable juice, horseradish, Worcestershire and hot pepper sauce. Serve over ice. Garnish with lemon slices.   *Makes 3 cups*

Hot 'n' Spicy Mocktail: Increase prepared horseradish to 1 tablespoon.

Mini Cheese-Tomato Napoleons

(photo on front cover)

Thaw/Prep Time: 40 minutes   **Bake Time:** 20 minutes

½ package (17¼-ounce size) **PEPPERIDGE FARM
Frozen Puff Pastry Sheets (1 sheet)**
¾ **cup shredded sharp Cheddar** *or* **feta cheese**
1 small tomato, diced (about ½ cup)

1. Thaw pastry sheet at room temperature 30 minutes. Preheat oven to 400°F.

2. Unfold pastry on lightly floured surface. Cut into 3 strips along fold marks. Cut each strip into 6 rectangles. Place 1 inch apart on baking sheet. Bake 15 minutes or until golden. Remove from baking sheet and cool on wire rack.

3. Split pastries into 2 layers making 36 layers in all. Place 18 bottom layers on baking sheet. Mix cheese and tomato. Top bottom layers with about **1 tablespoon** cheese mixture and top layers. Bake at 400°F. for 5 minutes or until warm.

Makes 18 napoleons

Variation: In Step 3 top cheese mixture with crumbled cooked bacon before baking.

Chili con Queso Bites

Prep Time: 10 minutes   **Cook Time:** 10 minutes

4 **eggs**
½ **cup PACE Picante Sauce** *or* **Thick & Chunky Salsa**
¼ **cup all-purpose flour**
2 **teaspoons chili powder**
1½ **cups shredded Cheddar cheese (6 ounces)**
1 **green onion, chopped (about 2 tablespoons)**

1. Preheat oven to 400°F. Grease 24 (3-inch) muffin-pan cups. Set aside.

2. In medium bowl mix eggs, picante sauce, flour and chili powder. Stir in cheese and onion.

3. Spoon about **1 tablespoon** cheese mixture into each cup. Bake 10 minutes or until golden brown. Serve warm or at room temperature with sour cream and additional picante sauce if desired.   *Makes 24 appetizers*

TIP

Baked appetizers may be frozen. To reheat,
bake frozen appetizers at 350°F. for 10 minutes
or until hot.

Left to right: *Bloody Mary Mocktails (page 60)
and Chili Con Queso Bites*

Mushroom Stuffing Balls

Prep Time: 25 minutes   **Cook Time:** 15 minutes

½ cup margarine *or* butter, melted
4 eggs, beaten
2 tablespoons chopped fresh parsley *or* 2 teaspoons dried parsley flakes
⅛ teaspoon garlic powder *or* 1 clove garlic, minced
2½ cups chopped mushrooms (about 8 ounces)
1 medium onion, chopped (about ½ cup)
½ cup grated Parmesan cheese
2½ cups PEPPERIDGE FARM Herb Seasoned Stuffing

1. Mix margarine, eggs, parsley, garlic powder, mushrooms, onion and cheese. Add stuffing. Mix lightly. Shape into 32 (1-inch) balls and place 2 inches apart on baking sheet.

2. Bake at 350°F. for 15 minutes or until golden.

Makes 32 appetizers

TIP

To make ahead, shape into balls and place on baking sheet. Freeze. When frozen, store in plastic bag up to 1 month. To bake, place frozen balls on baking sheet and bake at 350°F. for 20 minutes or until golden.

Left to right: *Mushroom Stuffing Balls and Party Meatballs (page 68)*

Brie en Croûte

Thaw/Prep Time: 45 minutes
Cook/Stand Time: 1 hour 20 minutes

½ package (17¼-ounce size) PEPPERIDGE FARM
   Frozen Puff Pastry Sheets (1 sheet)
1 egg
1 tablespoon water
¼ cup toasted sliced almonds (optional)
¼ cup chopped fresh parsley
1 Brie cheese round (about 1 pound)
   PEPPERIDGE FARM Water Crackers

1. Thaw pastry sheet at room temperature 30 minutes. Preheat oven to 400°F. Mix egg and water and set aside.

2. Unfold pastry on lightly floured surface. Roll into 14-inch square. Cut off corners to make a circle. Sprinkle almonds and parsley in center of circle. Top with cheese. Brush edge of circle with egg mixture. Fold two opposite sides over cheese. Trim remaining two sides to 2-inches from edge of cheese. Fold these two sides onto the round. Press edges to seal. Place seam-side down on baking sheet. Decorate top with pastry scraps if desired. Brush with egg mixture.

3. Bake 20 minutes or until golden. Let stand 1 hour. Serve with crackers. *Serves 12*

Top to bottom: *Spanikopitas (page 69) and Brie en Croûte*

Party Meatballs

(photo on page 65)

Prep Time: 20 minutes   **Cook Time:** 25 minutes

   1 can (11⅛ ounces) CAMPBELL'S Condensed Italian
       Tomato Soup
   1 pound ground beef
  ¼ cup dry bread crumbs
   1 egg, beaten
   1 tablespoon Worcestershire sauce
  ½ cup water
   2 tablespoons vinegar
   2 teaspoons packed brown sugar

1. Mix ¼ *cup* soup, beef, bread crumbs, egg and Worcestershire *thoroughly* and shape *firmly* into 48 (½-inch) meatballs. Arrange in 15- by 10-inch jelly-roll pan.

2. Bake at 350°F. for 15 minutes or until meatballs are no longer pink.

3. In large saucepan mix remaining soup, water, vinegar and sugar. Over medium heat, heat to a boil. Reduce heat to low. Cover and cook 5 minutes. Add meatballs and heat through.

Makes 48 appetizers

Party Frankfurters: Substitute 1 pound frankfurters, cut into 1-inch pieces for meatballs. In step 3 add frankfurters with soup.

TIP

To shape meatballs, shape meat mixture into an
8- by 6-inch rectangle. Cut into 48 squares.
Roll into meatballs.

Spanikopitas

(photo on page 67)
Thaw/Prep Time: 45 minutes   **Cook Time:** 20 minutes

1 package (17¼ ounces) PEPPERIDGE FARM Frozen
    Puff Pastry Sheets (2 sheets)
3 eggs
1 tablespoon water
½ cup crumbled feta cheese (2 ounces)
1 package (about 10 ounces) frozen chopped
    spinach, thawed and *well drained*
1 medium onion, finely chopped (about ½ cup)
2 tablespoons chopped fresh parsley

1. Thaw pastry sheets at room temperature 30 minutes. Preheat oven to 400°F. Mix *1* egg and water and set aside. Mix remaining eggs, cheese, spinach, onion and parsley and set aside.

2. Unfold pastry on lightly floured surface. Roll each sheet into a 12-inch square and cut each into 16 (3-inch) squares. Place *1 tablespoon* spinach mixture in center of each square. Brush edges of squares with egg mixture. Fold squares to form triangles. Press edges to seal. Place 2 inches apart on baking sheet. Brush with egg mixture.

3. Bake 20 minutes or until golden. Serve warm or at room temperature.

Makes 32 appetizers

Two Cheese Party Pastries

Thaw/Bake Time: 45 minutes   **Prep/Chill Time:** 35 minutes

½ package (17¼-ounce size) PEPPERIDGE FARM
Frozen Puff Pastry Sheets (1 sheet)
1½ cups crumbled blue cheese (about 6 ounces)
½ package (8-ounce size) cream cheese, softened
¼ cup heavy cream
1 teaspoon lemon juice
¼ cup walnuts, chopped
Chopped fresh parsley
1 medium Granny Smith apple, thinly sliced

1. Thaw pastry sheet at room temperature 30 minutes. Preheat oven to 400°F.

2. Unfold pastry on lightly floured surface. Cut into 3 strips along fold marks. Cut each strip into 6 rectangles. Place 2 inches apart on baking sheet. Bake 15 minutes or until golden. Remove from baking sheet. Cool on wire rack.

3. In medium bowl with electric mixer at low speed, beat blue cheese, cream cheese, cream and lemon juice until smooth.

4. Split pastries into 2 layers. Spread 18 halves with *1 tablespoon* cheese mixture. Top with remaining halves and spread with remaining cheese mixture. Sprinkle with walnuts and parsley. Top each pastry with *1* apple slice. Chill before serving.

Makes 18 pastries

Top to bottom: *Ham and Cheese Stromboli (page 74)
and Two Cheese Party Pastries*

Chocolate Walnut Strudel

Thaw/Prep Time: 45 minutes   **Cook/Cool Time:** 1 hour 5 minutes

½ package (17¼-ounce size) **PEPPERIDGE FARM Frozen Puff Pastry Sheets (1 sheet)**
1 **egg**
1 **tablespoon water**
4 **squares (1 ounce** *each*) **semi-sweet chocolate**
2 **tablespoons milk**
1 **tablespoon margarine** *or* **butter**
½ **cup chopped walnuts**
Sweetened whipped cream

1. Thaw pastry sheet at room temperature 30 minutes. Preheat oven to 375°F. Mix egg and water and set aside.

2. In large microwave-safe bowl microwave chocolate, milk and margarine on HIGH 1½ minutes or until chocolate is almost melted, stirring halfway through heating. Stir until chocolate is completely melted.

3. Unfold pastry on lightly floured surface. Roll into 16- by 12-inch rectangle. Spread chocolate mixture evenly on pastry to within 1½ inches of edges. Sprinkle walnuts over chocolate. Starting at short side, roll up like a jelly roll. Place seam-side down on baking sheet. Tuck ends under to seal. Brush with egg mixture.

4. Bake 35 minutes or until golden. Cool on baking sheet on wire rack at least 30 minutes. Slice and serve with whipped cream.

Serves 8

Top to bottom: *Chocolate Bundles (page 75)
and Chocolate Walnut Strudel*

Ham & Cheese Stromboli

(photo on page 71)
Thaw/Prep Time: 45 minutes   **Cook Time:** 25 minutes

½ package (17¼-ounce size) PEPPERIDGE FARM
Frozen Puff Pastry Sheets (1 sheet)
1 egg
1 tablespoon water
½ pound sliced cooked ham
½ pound sliced cooked turkey
1 cup shredded Cheddar cheese (4 ounces)

1. Thaw pastry sheet at room temperature 30 minutes. Preheat oven to 400°F. Mix egg and water and set aside.

2. Unfold pastry on lightly floured surface. Roll into 16- by 12-inch rectangle. With short side facing you, layer ham and turkey on bottom half of pastry to within 1 inch of edges. Sprinkle meat with cheese. Starting at short side, roll up like a jelly roll. Place seam-side down on baking sheet. Tuck ends under to seal. Brush with egg mixture.

3. Bake 25 minutes or until golden. Slice and serve warm.

Serves 6

Chocolate Bundles

(photo on page 73)

Thaw/Prep Time: 45 minutes   **Cook/Cool Time:** 25 minutes

½ package (17¼-ounce size) **PEPPERIDGE FARM
Frozen Puff Pastry sheets (1 sheet)**
1 package (6 ounces) semi-sweet chocolate pieces
¼ cup chopped walnuts
Confectioners' sugar

1. Thaw pastry sheet at room temperature 30 minutes. Preheat oven to 400°F. Mix chocolate pieces and walnuts and set aside.

2. Unfold pastry on lightly floured surface. Roll into 12-inch square. Cut into 9 (4-inch) squares. Place about **2 tablespoons** chocolate mixture in center of each square. Brush edges of squares with water. Fold corners to center on top of filling and twist tightly to seal. Fan out corners. Place 2 inches apart on baking sheet.

3. Bake 15 minutes or until golden. Remove from baking sheet. Cool on wire rack 10 minutes. Sprinkle with confectioners' sugar.

Makes 9 bundles

TIP

For large bundles, cut pastry into 4 (6-inch) squares and place about ⅓ **cup** chocolate mixture in center of each. Proceed as in step 2. *Makes 4 bundles*

Tomato Soup Spice Cake

Prep Time: 10 minutes   **Cook Time:** 35 minutes

        1 package (about 18 ounces) spice cake mix
        1 can (10¾ ounces) CAMPBELL'S Condensed Tomato
          Soup
      ½ cup water
        2 eggs
          Cream Cheese Frosting (recipe follows)

1. Preheat oven to 350°F. Grease and lightly flour two 8- or 9-inch round cake pans.

2. In large bowl mix cake mix, soup, water and eggs according to package directions.

3. Pour into prepared pans. Bake 25 minutes or until toothpick inserted in center comes out clean.

4. Cool on wire racks 10 minutes. Remove from pans and cool completely on wire racks.

5. Fill and frost with Cream Cheese Frosting.   *Serves 12*

Cream Cheese Frosting: Beat 2 packages (3 ounces *each*) softened cream cheese until smooth. Gradually blend in 1 package (1 pound) sifted confectioners' sugar and ½ teaspoon vanilla extract. If desired, thin with milk.

Tomato Soup Spice Cake

Campbell's
FOOTBALL FAN FARE

Beef Taco Bake

Prep Time: 10 minutes   **Cook Time:** 30 minutes

> 1 **pound ground beef**
> 1 **can (10¾ ounces) CAMPBELL'S Condensed Tomato Soup**
> 1 **cup PACE Thick & Chunky Salsa *or* Picante Sauce**
> ½ **cup milk**
> 6 **flour tortillas (8-inch) *or* 8 corn tortillas (6-inch), cut into 1-inch pieces**
> 1 **cup shredded Cheddar cheese (4 ounces)**

1. In medium skillet over medium-high heat, cook beef until browned, stirring to separate meat. Pour off fat.

2. Add soup, salsa, milk, tortillas and *half* the cheese. Spoon into 2-quart shallow baking dish. ***Cover.***

3. Bake at 400°F. for 30 minutes or until hot. Sprinkle with remaining cheese.

Serves 4

Beef Taco Bake

King Ranch Turkey Casserole

Prep Time: 15 minutes   **Cook Time:** 40 minutes

> 1 can (10¾ ounces) CAMPBELL'S Condensed Cream
> of Mushroom Soup *or* 98% Fat Free Cream of
> Mushroom Soup
> ¾ cup PACE Picante Sauce
> ¾ cup sour cream
> 1 tablespoon chili powder
> 2 medium tomatoes, chopped (about 2 cups)
> 3 cups cubed cooked turkey *or* chicken
> 12 corn tortillas (6-inch), cut into 1-inch pieces
> 1 cup shredded Cheddar cheese (4 ounces)
> Green onion for garnish

1. Mix soup, picante sauce, sour cream, chili powder, tomatoes and turkey.

2. In 2-quart shallow baking dish arrange *half* the tortilla pieces. Top with *half* the turkey mixture. Repeat layers. Sprinkle with cheese.

3. Bake at 350°F. for 40 minutes or until hot. Serve with additional picante sauce and sour cream. Garnish with green onion.

Serves 8

King Ranch Turkey Casserole

Creamy Chicken & Cheese Enchiladas

Prep Time: 20 minutes   **Cook Time:** 40 minutes

1 can (10¾ ounces) CAMPBELL'S Condensed Cream of Chicken Soup *or* 98% Fat Free Cream of Chicken Soup

1 container (8 ounces) sour cream

1 cup PACE Picante Sauce *or* Thick & Chunky Salsa

2 teaspoons chili powder

2 cups chopped cooked chicken

1 cup shredded Monterey Jack cheese (4 ounces)

12 flour tortillas (6-inch)

1 medium tomato, chopped (about 1 cup)

1 green onion, sliced (about 2 tablespoons)

1. Mix soup, sour cream, picante sauce and chili powder.

2. Mix *1 cup* soup mixture, chicken and cheese.

3. Along one side of each tortilla, spread about ¼ *cup* chicken mixture. Roll up each tortilla around filling and place seam-side down in 3-quart shallow baking dish.

4. Spread remaining soup mixture over enchiladas. Cover and bake at 350°F. for 40 minutes or until hot. Top with tomato and onion.

Serves 6

TIP

For 2 cups chopped cooked chicken, in medium saucepan over medium heat, in 4 cups boiling water, cook 1 pound skinless, boneless chicken breasts **or** thighs, cubed, 5 minutes or until chicken is no longer pink. Drain and chop chicken.

Top to bottom: *Turkey Enchiladas (page 86) and Creamy Chicken and Cheese Enchiladas*

Nachos Grande

Prep Time: 10 minutes   **Cook Time:** 10 minutes

1 can (11 ounces) CAMPBELL'S Condensed Fiesta
    Nacho Cheese Soup
⅓ cup milk
1 pound ground beef
1 small onion, chopped (about ¼ cup)
5 cups tortilla chips (about 5 ounces)
1 medium tomato, chopped (about 1 cup)
1 jalapeño pepper, seeded and sliced (optional)

1. In small saucepan mix soup and milk. Set aside.

2. In medium skillet over medium-high heat, cook beef and onion until beef is browned, stirring to separate meat. Pour off fat. Add **½ cup** soup mixture. Reduce heat to low and heat through.

3. Over medium heat, heat remaining soup mixture, stirring often.

4. Arrange chips on large platter and top with meat mixture. Spoon soup mixture over meat. Top with tomato and pepper.

Serves 8 as an appetizer

*Top to bottom: Nachos Grande
and Nacho Tacos (page 87)*

Turkey Enchiladas

(photo on page 83)
Prep Time: 25 minutes   **Cook Time:** 25 minutes

1 can (10¾ ounces) CAMPBELL'S Condensed Cream
    of Celery Soup *or* 98% Fat Free Cream of Celery
    Soup
½ cup sour cream
2 tablespoons margarine *or* butter
1 medium onion, chopped (about ½ cup)
1 teaspoon chili powder
2 cups chopped cooked turkey *or* chicken
1 can (4 ounces) chopped green chilies
8 flour tortillas (8-inch)
1 cup shredded Cheddar *or* Monterey Jack cheese
    (4 ounces)

1. In small bowl mix soup and sour cream and set aside.

2. In medium saucepan over medium heat, heat margarine. Add onion and chili powder and cook until tender. Add turkey, chilies and *2 tablespoons* soup mixture.

3. Spread *½ cup* soup mixture in 2-quart shallow baking dish. Along one side of each tortilla, spread about *¼ cup* turkey mixture. Roll up each tortilla around filling and place seam-side down in baking dish.

4. Spread remaining soup mixture over enchiladas. Sprinkle cheese over soup mixture. Bake at 350°F. for 25 minutes or until hot.

Serves 4

Nacho Tacos

(photo on page 85)

Prep Time: 10 minutes   **Cook Time:** 10 minutes

    1 **pound ground beef**
    1 **medium onion, chopped (about ½ cup)**
    ½ **teaspoon chili powder**
    1 **can (11 ounces) CAMPBELL'S Condensed Fiesta
       Nacho Cheese Soup**
    8 **taco shells**
    1 **cup shredded lettuce**
    1 **medium tomato, chopped (about 1 cup)**

1. In medium skillet over medium-high heat, cook beef, onion and chili powder until beef is browned, stirring to separate meat. Pour off fat.

2. Add **½ cup** soup and heat through.

3. In small saucepan over low heat, heat remaining soup until hot. Divide meat mixture among taco shells. Top with **1½ tablespoons** hot soup, lettuce and tomato.   *Makes 8 tacos*

Pronto Pizza

Prep Time: 10 minutes   **Cook Time:** 12 minutes

¾ cup **PREGO Traditional Pasta Sauce** *or* **Extra
Chunky Tomato, Onion & Garlic Pasta Sauce**
1 **Italian bread shell (about 16 ounces)**
1½ **cups shredded mozzarella cheese (6 ounces)**

Preheat oven to 425°F. Spread pasta sauce over shell to edge. Top with cheese. Bake 12 minutes or until cheese is melted.

Serves 4

TIP

Top with thinly sliced pepperoni, crumbled cooked ground beef *or* bulk pork sausage, chopped green pepper, canned sliced mushrooms, drained, *or* grated Parmesan cheese before baking.

Pronto Pizza

Vegetable Tortilla Triangles

(photo on front cover)

Prep Time: 15 minutes   **Cook Time:** 10 minutes

- 1 can (10¾ ounces) CAMPBELL'S HEALTHY REQUEST Condensed Cream of Celery Soup
- 1 medium tomato, chopped (about 1 cup)
- 1 small green pepper, chopped (about ½ cup)
- 2 green onions, sliced (about ¼ cup)
- 1 jalapeño pepper, seeded and finely chopped (optional)
- 8 flour tortillas (8-inch)
- 1 cup shredded Cheddar cheese (4 ounces)

1. Mix soup, tomato, green pepper, onions and jalapeño pepper.

2. Place tortillas on 2 baking sheets. Top each tortilla with ⅓ *cup* soup mixture. Spread to within ½ inch of edge. Top with cheese.

3. Bake at 400°F. for 10 minutes or until tortillas are crisp. Cut each into quarters.   *Makes 32 appetizers*

Nutritional Values per Serving: Calories 59, Total Fat 2g, Saturated Fat 1g, Cholesterol 4mg, Sodium 142mg, Total Carbohydrate 8g, Protein 2g

Product Index

Recipe Index

Metric Conversion Chart

VOLUME MEASUREMENTS (dry)

1/8 teaspoon = 0.5 mL
1/4 teaspoon = 1 mL
1/2 teaspoon = 2 mL
3/4 teaspoon = 4 mL
1 teaspoon = 5 mL
1 tablespoon = 15 mL
2 tablespoons = 30 mL
1/4 cup = 60 mL
1/3 cup = 75 mL
1/2 cup = 125 mL
2/3 cup = 150 mL
3/4 cup = 175 mL
1 cup = 250 mL
2 cups = 1 pint = 500 mL
3 cups = 750 mL
4 cups = 1 quart = 1 L

VOLUME MEASUREMENTS (fluid)

1 fluid ounce (2 tablespoons) = 30 mL
4 fluid ounces (1/2 cup) = 125 mL
8 fluid ounces (1 cup) = 250 mL
12 fluid ounces (1 1/2 cups) = 375 mL
16 fluid ounces (2 cups) = 500 mL

WEIGHTS (mass)

1/2 ounce = 15 g
1 ounce = 30 g
3 ounces = 90 g
4 ounces = 120 g
8 ounces = 225 g
10 ounces = 285 g
12 ounces = 360 g
16 ounces = 1 pound = 450 g

DIMENSIONS

1/16 inch = 2 mm
1/8 inch = 3 mm
1/4 inch = 6 mm
1/2 inch = 1.5 cm
3/4 inch = 2 cm
1 inch = 2.5 cm

OVEN TEMPERATURES

250°F = 120°C
275°F = 140°C
300°F = 150°C
325°F = 160°C
350°F = 180°C
375°F = 190°C
400°F = 200°C
425°F = 220°C
450°F = 230°C

BAKING PAN SIZES

Utensil	Size in Inches/Quarts	Metric Volume	Size in Centimeters
Baking or	8×8×2	2 L	20×20×5
Cake Pan	9×9×2	2.5 L	23×23×5
(square or	12×8×2	3 L	30×20×5
rectangular)	13×9×2	3.5 L	33×23×5
Loaf Pan	8×4×3	1.5 L	20×10×7
	9×5×3	2 L	23×13×7
Round Layer	8×1½	1.2 L	20×4
Cake Pan	9×1½	1.5 L	23×4
Pie Plate	8×1¼	750 mL	20×3
	9×1¼	1 L	23×3
Baking Dish	1 quart	1 L	—
or Casserole	1½ quart	1.5 L	—
	2 quart	2 L	—